My Bible Story Book

Carine Mackenzie
Illustrated by Fred Apps

CF4·K

Contents

Stories from
the Old Testament

1. God made the world

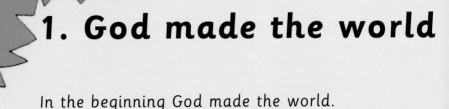

In the beginning God made the world.

He made the sun and the moon and the stars in the sky. He made the mountains, and rivers.

He made the birds and insects, fish and animals.

God saw that it was all very good.

Everything God does
is good.

God made people too. He made Adam from the dust of the ground. He made Eve his wife from one of his ribs.

God gave them a beautiful garden to live in.

Everything was perfect.

God is King of Creation.

One day Adam and Eve disobeyed God.

God had told them not to eat the fruit from one tree in the middle of the garden.

But Eve listened to the devil and ate some of the fruit. She gave some to Adam. He ate it too.

Life was no longer perfect.

Sin spoiled everything.

Sin destroyed God's perfect world. All have sinned.

2. Noah

God told Noah to build a big boat called an ark. 'I will send a flood to destroy the wicked people in the world,' he said. Noah built the ark just as God said.

Sin must be punished.

When the ark was finished, God told Noah to take two of every kind of animal into the ark and seven of some other kinds of animals.

Noah and his wife and his three sons and their wives all went into the ark.

God closed the door.

God wants to save his people from their sins.

It rained for 40 days and 40 nights. The earth was flooded, even the mountains were covered, but Noah and his family were safe in the ark.

God gave the rainbow as a sign of his promise never to destroy the world with a flood.

God always keeps his promises.

3. Isaac

Abraham and Sarah were very old.

They had given up hope of having a baby.

But God had promised they would have a son.

When Isaac was born, Abraham and Sarah were so pleased.

They made a great feast to celebrate.

God wants to bless you and give you good things.

Isaac's father sent a servant to a far country to find a wife for Isaac.
The servant prayed to God for help.

A beautiful and helpful girl called Rebekah agreed to marry Isaac.

Isaac was delighted when he met her.

He loved her very much.

God's plans are perfect.

Isaac and Rebekah had twin babies, Esau and Jacob. They did not look alike. When they grew up Esau liked to hunt but Jacob liked to stay at home near the tents. Jacob and Esau were not friendly with each other. Jacob tricked Esau out of his blessing. But God was still in control.

God is in charge, always.

4. Joseph

Joseph had ten older brothers and one younger brother, but Joseph was his father Jacob's favourite.

Jacob gave Joseph a brightly coloured coat.

Joseph dreamed that he was going to be more important than all his brothers. He dreamt that he would be more important than his older brothers and even his father.

Joseph's brothers became angry and jealous.

Thank God for loving you. God is love.

One day they pounced on Joseph and threw him into a deep pit. They sold him to some merchants who were on their way to Egypt. Joseph became a slave, working hard for his master.

He was thrown into prison because someone told a lie about him. But God was with Joseph all the time.

God is with you. You can trust in him.

Pharaoh, the king, discovered how wise Joseph was and let him out of prison. Joseph was put in charge of all the grain in Egypt. He made sure there was enough food for everyone during hard times.

Joseph's brothers came to Egypt. There was very little to eat in their country. They needed to buy food. The brothers bowed down to Joseph. Joseph's dream came true. God's plan to save Joseph's family came true as well.

God's plan to save his people from sin came true when Jesus died on the cross.

5. Moses

God's people became slaves in Egypt. The new king was very cruel; he wanted to kill all the boy babies.

A little baby boy was born in one family. The mother thought of a plan to save him. She made a basket of reeds, put the baby inside and placed the basket in the river.

God is with us even in dangerous times.

A princess found the basket.

When she saw the little baby crying, she took pity on him. She called the baby Moses.

No harm came to Moses.

His mother was called and the princess paid her to look after him.

God can rescue you too. We all need to be saved from sin.

Moses had a special work to do when he grew up. With God's help he led his people out of Egypt. They crossed the Red Sea and travelled to the country that God had promised them. Moses had lots of adventures on the way - but he never arrived at the promised land himself.

God helps his people to do his work. God's work is the best work to do.

6. Joshua

Joshua became the leader of the people after Moses.

He was a very brave soldier.

God helped him too.

When they had to cross the river Jordan, God made the water stop and they all walked over on dry land.

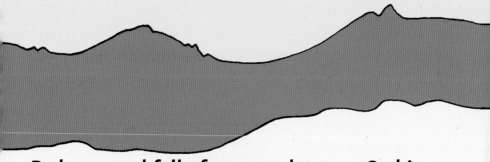

Be brave and full of courage because God is with you. Don't be afraid.

Joshua led the army against the city of Jericho.

God told him what to do and he obeyed.

They marched round the city walls once a day for six days. On the seventh day they marched round seven times, blowing trumpets.

Obey God. He knows the best thing to do.

The walls of the city fell down flat.

The soldiers were able to walk straight in and take the city.

With God's help Joshua and the people of Israel won the battle of Jericho.

God will help you.

He knows what you need.

7. Ruth

Ruth was a young widow from Moab. Ruth loved the Lord God. She was kind to Naomi her mother-in-law.

Naomi's husband was also dead. When Naomi decided to go back to Bethlehem Ruth wanted to go with her.

'Do not ask me to leave you,' begged Ruth.

'Your people will be my people. Your God will be my God.'

God is the only true God.

Ruth and Naomi travelled to Bethlehem at harvest-time.

Ruth went to work in a field belonging to Boaz.

She picked up the grain that was dropped.

Boaz was kind to her.

He gave her food and drink.

Boaz told his men to 'Drop some grain on purpose for her.'

God gives you food and drink. He gives you all you need.

Naomi told Ruth to go and visit Boaz. He was a relative and would help them.

Ruth went to the threshing floor where the harvest grain was stored.

She asked Boaz to buy back their family land. Boaz was pleased to help.

Ruth and Boaz were married.

They had a baby son Obed.

Obed became the grandfather of King David.

God loves us.

Tell him how lovely he is.

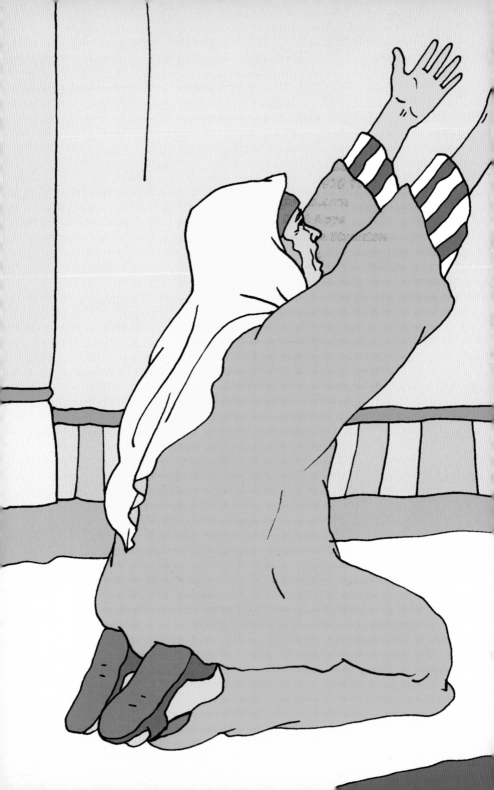

8. Samuel

Hannah wanted a baby so much.

She prayed to God, asking him for a baby son.

'I will give him back to work for God,' she said.

God answered her prayer.

A baby was born.

Hannah called him Samuel.

Samuel's name means 'asked of God.'

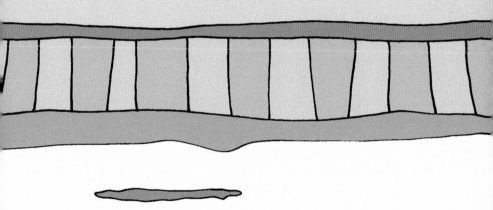

You can speak to God any time, anywhere.

When Samuel was a little older, he went to the temple to work for God. He helped the old priest Eli.

His mother and father would visit him every year.

His mother brought him new clothes each time.

It doesn't matter how old you are Jesus wants you to follow him.

One night, as he lay in bed, Samuel heard a voice calling his name, 'Samuel! Samuel!'

He thought it was Eli at first.

At last Eli realised that God was calling Samuel.

He told Samuel what to say.

'Speak, Lord, for your servant is listening.'

God spoke to Samuel.

God wants you to listen to him and obey.

9. David

David was the youngest in his family. He was good looking and loved to play the harp. He also looked after his father's sheep. He took them to find grass to eat and water to drink.

He protected them from wild animals. He even killed a lion and a bear who attacked his flock.

Jesus cares for us just as a shepherd cares for his sheep.

Goliath was a huge giant who fought against the people of Israel.

The soldiers were afraid of him.

David's brothers were soldiers.

One day David's father told him to visit his

brothers at the army camp.

When David saw and heard Goliath he said,

'I will fight him! God will help me just as he helped me against the lion and the bear.'

When people hurt us or upset us God can help and comfort us.

David took five smooth stones from the river and using the shepherd's sling he took aim against Goliath.

The first stone hit Goliath on the forehead.

He fell down dead.

With God's help, David had saved his people from their enemy.

God can help us to do great things for him.

10. Elijah

Elijah loved God.

He had to hide from wicked King Ahab.

He drank water from the river.

Every morning and evening, ravens brought bread and meat for him to eat. God was looking after Elijah.

God cares for you day after day.

The country needed rain.

The river dried up.

Elijah went into a town.

He spoke to a widow woman gathering sticks.

'Please give me some water and a piece of bread,' he asked.

Jesus is called 'The water of life.' He gives life to your soul.

I just have a handful of flour and a little oil in a jar,'
the widow woman said. 'There is only enough for one
last meal for me and my son.'

'Make me some cake first,' said Elijah. 'God will look
after you.'

The widow woman did as she was asked and her jar of
oil did not run dry and the bin of flour was not used up.

The lady, her son and Elijah had plenty to eat.

Thank God for your food.

Every good gift comes from him.

11. Elisha

Elisha was a man of God.

As he travelled around the country, he often visited a lady and her husband.

They made him a special room with a bed, a table, a chair and a lamp.

**Do what you can to help people
who love and work for God.**

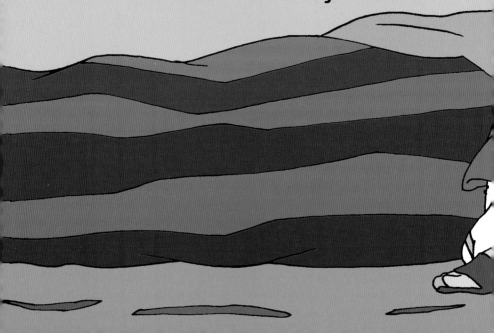

One day Elisha gave the lady good news. 'By this time next year you will have a baby son.'

The lady was so pleased. She had been wanting a baby for a long time.

When the little boy grew old enough he would go out to his father's fields to watch the men working.

God always answers our prayers.

Sometimes he says yes, no or wait.

One day the young boy ran to his father calling out, 'My head, my head.'

Someone carried him to his mother and he died in her lap. The lady sent for Elisha.

He prayed to God and life returned to the little boy.

He sat up and sneezed seven times.

**Even when problems seem very big
pray to God about them.
He can help you.**

12. Daniel

Daniel prayed to God every day.

Some bad men did not like Daniel.

They made the king pass a bad law.

Anyone who prayed to God was to be put into a den of lions.

Pray to God even if other people do not. God is real and true.

Daniel loved God. He still prayed to him.

So Daniel was grabbed and put into the den with the lions.

However, God took care of Daniel.

The mouths of the lions were closed.

The lions did not harm Daniel at all.

God takes care of you when you are scared and when you are not scared.

The king came next morning to see what had happened to Daniel. He called out. The king was so pleased when Daniel answered him.

Daniel was safe because he had trusted in God.

Even the king now knew that Daniel's God was the true God.

Tell others about Jesus.
They need to know him too.

13. Jonah

God told Jonah to go to a far away town to tell the people about him. But Jonah did not do what God asked.

He ran away in the other direction.

Jonah got on a boat and then God sent a great storm.

Nobody can hide from God. He knows everything and everyone.

The boat was tossed about.

All the sailors were frightened.

They knew Jonah was running away from God's work so they threw him overboard.

God sent a huge fish to swallow Jonah.

Jonah prayed to God from inside the fish.

God hears you
wherever you are.

The big fish spat Jonah out on to dry land.

God had used the fish to save Jonah.

Jonah then went to the town to tell the people about God. They listened to him and turned away from their sins.

All people need to know they are sinners.

All people need to know that God can save.

Stories from
the New Testament

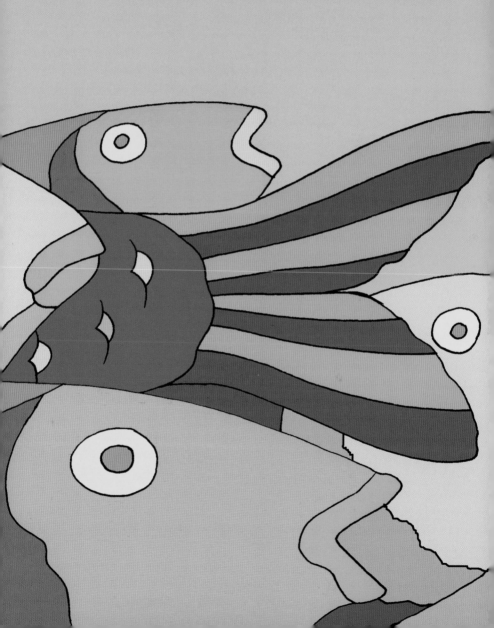

14. The birth of Jesus

Mary and Joseph had to go to Bethlehem. There was no room for them in the inn. When Mary's baby was born she made a bed for him in a manger, the animal's feeding box. Joseph looked after him like a father but Jesus' real Father was God. God told Joseph to call the baby JESUS, which means Saviour.

**God sent Jesus, his only son,
to save his people from their sin.**

Shepherds were out in the field looking after their sheep at night. An angel came to tell them that Jesus the Saviour had been born. Many angels filled the sky, praising God. The shepherds hurried to Bethlehem to see Jesus.

We should praise God. We should tell him he is wonderful.

When Jesus was born, wise men saw a special star in the sky. They made a long journey to come and visit the special baby. The star led them on the way. They brought presents to the baby Jesus – gold, frankincense and myrrh. They knew that Jesus was the Son of God and they worshipped him.

Really wise people
trust in Jesus.

15. Jesus the boy

Mary and Joseph took Jesus to the temple in Jerusalem when he was very young. A good man called Simeon was delighted to hold the young Jesus in his arms. He knew he was the Saviour.

An old lady, Anna, who was always in the temple thanked God for Jesus the Saviour.

Read the Bible. Pray every day.
We need to spend time with God.

Jesus grew up in the town of Nazareth.

His father was a carpenter.

He had brothers and sisters.

He grew strong and wise.

When he was twelve years old he and his parents travelled to Jerusalem for a special feast.

On the way home Mary and Joseph could not find Jesus.

**Jesus was a child just like you,
but he never sinned.**

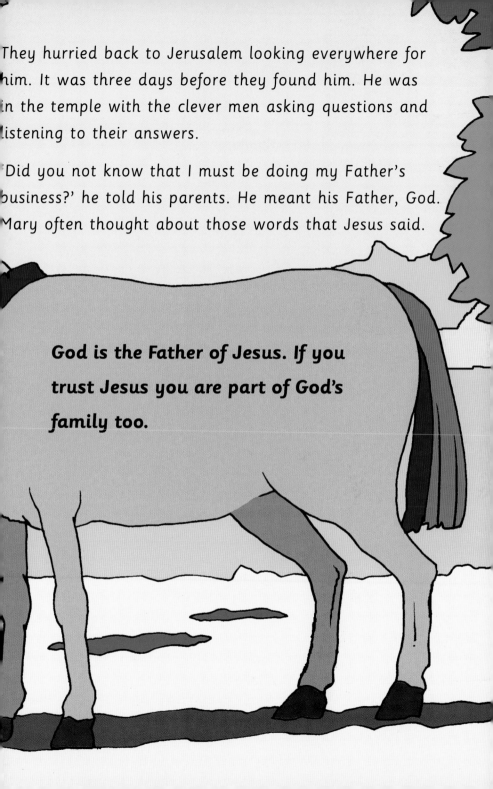

They hurried back to Jerusalem looking everywhere for him. It was three days before they found him. He was in the temple with the clever men asking questions and listening to their answers.

'Did you not know that I must be doing my Father's business?' he told his parents. He meant his Father, God. Mary often thought about those words that Jesus said.

God is the Father of Jesus. If you trust Jesus you are part of God's family too.

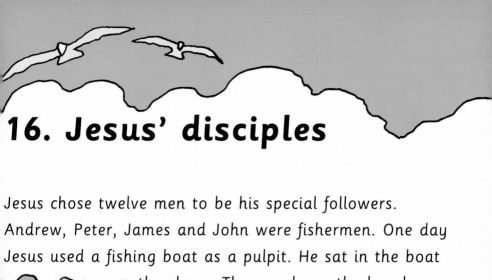

16. Jesus' disciples

Jesus chose twelve men to be his special followers. Andrew, Peter, James and John were fishermen. One day Jesus used a fishing boat as a pulpit. He sat in the boat near the shore. The people on the beach listened to him preaching.

Follow Jesus. Trust in him and obey him.

Jesus told Peter, 'Push your boat out further and put down your nets to catch some fish.'

'We have been working all night,' replied Peter, 'and have caught nothing. But we will do as you say.'

They caught so many fish, the net began to break. They called for the other ships to help. They were all amazed.

We must do as Jesus says. He wants what is best for us.

Jesus and his disciples were crossing the Sea of Galilee in a little boat when Jesus fell asleep. Suddenly a wild storm blew up. The waves lashed the boat. The disciples were scared. They woke Jesus in alarm.

'Peace, be still' he said to the wind and waves.

The sea was immediately calm.

Even the wind and the waves obey Jesus. He is all-powerful.

17. The children and Jesus

Some children were brought to Jesus, so that he would bless them. The disciples wanted to send them away. But Jesus said 'Let the children come to me. Don't stop them The kingdom of heaven belongs to them and others like them.' Jesus put his hands on them and blessed them.

Jesus loves children.
Jesus loves you.

Jesus was called urgently to the home of a little girl.

She was very ill. Her father believed Jesus could heal her. The little girl died.

Jesus went into her room with her mother and father.

'Get up' he said to her. She sat up in bed. Jesus had made her better. 'Give her something to eat' he said.

Jesus can even cure sickness.

He has power over illness.

A little boy went out to the countryside with a picnic of five barley loaves and two small fish. A huge crowd of people were there listening to Jesus preach. The crowd needed food to eat. Jesus used the little boy's food to feed the whole crowd. Jesus gave thanks to God. He kept on handing out the food till everyone had enough.

Jesus is amazing. He has power over big things and little things.

18. The loving father

Jesus told a story about a man who had two sons. The younger one said to his father, 'Give me my share of your money.' The father gave him the money and the young man left home. He went far away and spent it all. Soon he was very poor and hungry.

God loves you
better than the
best father.

He got a job looking after pigs. He was so hungry he felt like eating the pigs' food. 'The servants in my father's house are better off than I am,' he thought. 'I will go back home, and ask to be made a servant there.' So he set off for home.

Sometimes God gives sad times and hard lessons because we need them.

His father noticed him coming in the distance. He ran to him welcoming him with open arms. He was so glad to see him again. The loving father did not make him a servant. Instead he gave him a lovely robe, a ring and sandals.

The father made a big party to celebrate his son's return.

God the Father forgives us when we come to trust in his Son Jesus Christ.

19. A kind man

Jesus told a story about a kind man, who helped a stranger.

A poor man lay badly hurt on a lonely road. He had been beaten up by thieves. One man came along but he hurried past on the other side of the road.

God knows
how we feel.
Jesus knows
what pain and
sorrow is.

Another man came along. He noticed the poor man but did not stop to help.

Then the kind man arrived.

He felt sorry for the injured man.

He bandaged his wounds. He lifted the man on to his donkey and brought him to an inn and took care of him there for the night.

We should care for all people who need our help.
Jesus loves sinners. He died for them.

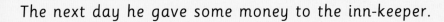

The next day he gave some money to the inn-keeper.

'Look after this man,' he said. 'If you need more money, I will repay you when I come back this way.'

Jesus tells us to be like the kind man.

Show others what Jesus is like by being loving and caring like Jesus.

20. Jesus heals

A poor lame man could not walk at all. Four of his friends decided to carry him on his mat to Jesus. The house was so crowded they could not get near. So they climbed up the outside stair to the roof, made a hole in it, and lowered the man down in front of Jesus. 'Your sins are forgiven' said Jesus. 'Pick up your mat and go home.' The man was completely cured.

Jesus has power over sin. He defeated sin when he died on the cross.

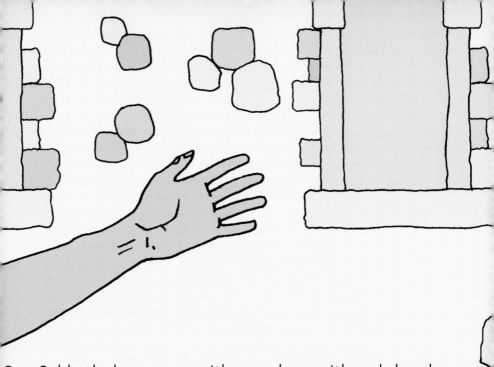

One Sabbath day a man with a useless, withered, hand met Jesus in the church.

'Stretch out your hand' Jesus commanded.

The man believed Jesus and obeyed him.

He stretched out his hand.

It was strong and useful again.

Jesus can heal. He has power over illness.
He can also give strength
to someone who is sick.

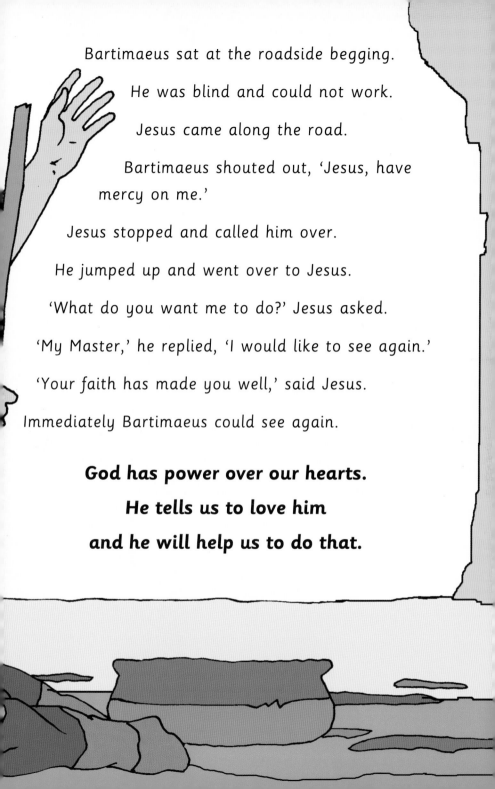

Bartimaeus sat at the roadside begging.

He was blind and could not work.

Jesus came along the road.

Bartimaeus shouted out, 'Jesus, have mercy on me.'

Jesus stopped and called him over.

He jumped up and went over to Jesus.

'What do you want me to do?' Jesus asked.

'My Master,' he replied, 'I would like to see again.'

'Your faith has made you well,' said Jesus.

Immediately Bartimaeus could see again.

God has power over our hearts.
He tells us to love him
and he will help us to do that.

21. The death of Jesus

Some people wanted to kill Jesus. Even his friends left him. He was nailed to a cross at Calvary and died. But this was part of God's plan. God is just and must punish sin. Jesus died so that those who love and trust him can have their sins forgiven.

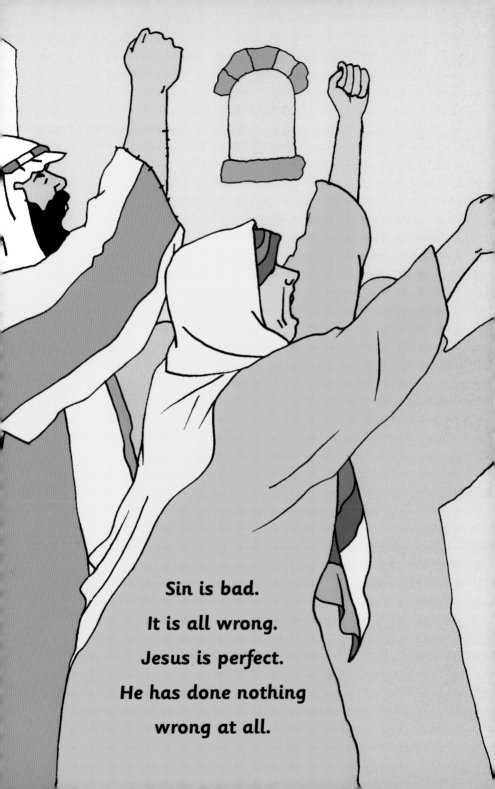

Sin is bad.
It is all wrong.
Jesus is perfect.
He has done nothing
wrong at all.

Jesus was buried in a tomb. A big stone was put over the entrance. Ladies came to visit the tomb. The big stone had been rolled away. The tomb was empty. Two angels gave them the good news, 'He is not here. He has risen.' The ladies rushed to tell Jesus' disciples.

Jesus is alive.

What wonderful news!

That evening the disciples were in a room with the doors firmly shut.

They were afraid, and worried. Jesus came and stood beside them.

'Peace be with you' he said.

He showed them his hands, which had been pierced with nails and his side, which had been cut with a spear. The disciples were so glad to see the Lord Jesus alive again.

Jesus is alive and loves you.

What a wonderful God we have.

22. The early church

Jesus was taken up to heaven but promised that God the Holy Spirit would help the dicsiples to tell others the good news of the gospel.

One day in Jerusalem a loud noise like a stormy wind filled the house. Tongues of fire rested on the head of each of the disciples. The Holy Spirit had come to help them.

Ask God for help to tell others about his Son, Jesus.

Peter was able to preach boldly about the Lord Jesus and the wonderful things he had done: he had died but God had raised him from the dead. About three thousand people that day turned from their sins to serve God; and many more in the days that followed.

Turn away from bad things.

Think about the Lord Jesus instead.

Peter and John went to the temple to pray. A lame man sat at the gate begging. He asked Peter and John for money.

Peter said, 'I have no silver or gold, but I will give you something else. Rise up and walk.'

He pulled him to his feet. The man could now walk for the first time. He walked into the temple, jumping for joy and praising God who had healed him.

23. Paul the missionary

Paul travelled to Damascus. He wanted to hurt the Christians who lived there. On the road a bright light from heaven flashed around him.

He fell to the ground. The Lord Jesus spoke to him.

Paul was led into Damascus. He was blind. He could not eat. Ananias was sent to help him. He laid his hands on Paul. He could see!

God has power over people who love him and over those who do not love him.

Paul's life was changed. He loved the Lord Jesus. He spent his time travelling to many countries, preaching about Jesus and setting up new churches. Some people heard the gospel gladly and believed.

Others threw stones at Paul and chased him out of town. Paul had many adventures.

Jesus can change your life. He can turn you away from sin. You will want to please God instead.

In the town of Philippi, Paul and his friend Silas were put in prison. They still prayed and sang praise to God.

God sent an earthquake to shake the prison. The jailor was afraid that his prisoners had escaped.

'What must I do to be saved?' he asked Paul.

Paul gave him the only answer for him and for his family and for us, 'Believe on the Lord Jesus and you will be saved.'

Believe in Jesus for everything about him is true.

24. Peter the Preacher

Dorcas was a kind Christian lady who lived in the seaside town of Joppa. She was good at sewing and made clothes for poor families. She fell ill and died. Her friends were so sad.

They sent for Peter and asked him to help.

He went to her room and prayed to God. 'Get up' he said. She opened her eyes and sat up. Her friends were delighted.

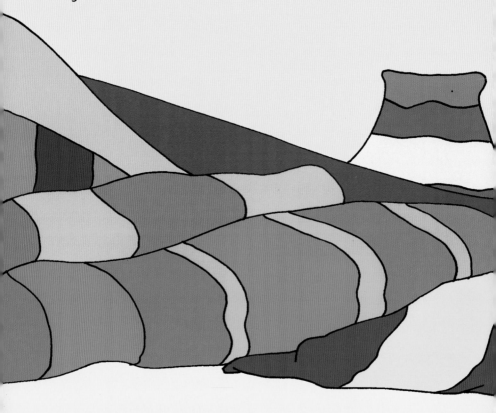

Jesus has power over death.
Nothing is stronger than him.

Herod the king was cruel to those who loved Jesus. He had Peter arrested and thrown into prison.

His Christian friends prayed for him.

One night an angel came and woke Peter up. 'Get up quickly' the angel said. The chains fell off his hands. 'Wrap your cloak around you and follow me.' The angel took him past the guards.

Then they went through the gate and out into the city.

It is good to pray for others. God answers prayer. He knows what needs to be done.

Peter made his way to the house of Mary, John Mark's mother. Many people were gathered there praying for Peter. He knocked at the door. Rhoda, a servant girl, went to answer. When she recognized Peter's voice, she forgot to open the door and rushed back to tell the others that Peter was there. No one believed her at first. Peter kept on knocking. Eventually they opened the door. Their prayers were wonderfully answered.

God answers prayer.
Thank him for this.

© Copyright 2006 Carine Mackenzie
ISBN: 978-1-84550-129-7
Reprinted in 2013
Published by Christian Focus Publications
Geanies House, Fearn, Tain, Ross-shire, IV20 1TW, Scotland, U.K.
www.christianfocus.com
Illustrated by Fred Apps
Cover design by Daniel van Straaten
Printed in China

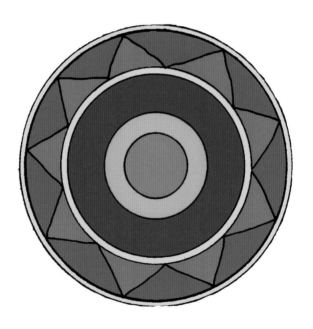